# THE APPALACHIAN TRAIL

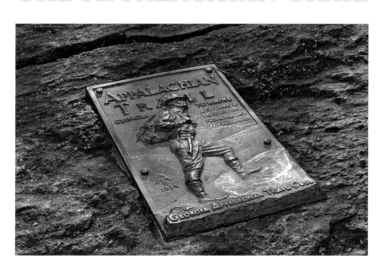

# THE APPALACHIAN TRAIL

## HIKING THE PEOPLE'S PATH

Foreword by RON J. TIPTON

Photography by BART SMITH

RIZZOLI
NEW YORK

APPALACHIAN TRAIL

# FOREWORD

The Appalachian Trail project has always been a love affair with the landscape of the eastern mountains—from its first acorn in Benton MacKaye's brain in the 1920s to the beloved mighty oak it has become. Today, the trail is commonly thought of as a hiking or backpacking destination or a place for status-free camaraderie for a few hours or even half a year. From the trillium at hikers' feet to the waves upon waves of smoky mountaintops as far as the eye can see, this storied footpath is also a place of healing, of restoration, of temporary retreat.

One of the trail's pioneers expressed this sentiment well nearly a century ago:

> *The purpose of the Appalachian Trail is to stimulate what Chauncey Hamlin refers to as an "outdoor culture." This means the study of*

*nature. And, it means the study of man. It means the study of man's place in nature. . . . We would plan specially for America. And, we would seek her spirit through direct contact, not through printer's ink. The outdoor culture is a contact culture. It seeks first-hand access to the forces, natural and human, which underlie our country; it places no reliance on a prating journalism. The Appalachian highland (which is within reach of half the nation's population) forms a background, still unspoiled, of American tradition. Its crestline marks a natural backbone for an American outdoor culture.*

Almost two decades later, once the original A.T. was in place, another trail-building pioneer put it in a less philosophical way closer to the hiker's experience: "The Trail itself seems age-old, so naturally does it fit into its surroundings. Just a path, now down a rough shoulder slope, now through old clearings sweet-scented with grasses in the sun, through dim forests, then up through scrub and out over bare mountain ledges, it seems it's been since the beginning; it seems it will be till the end."

The culture of today's Appalachian Trail is indeed a "contact culture": contact with nature, contact with each other. And landscape conservation of course requires that contact, that conversation—among hikers, the federal and state agencies that purchase lands to protect the trail's scenic values, the adjacent landowners, and the community at large. Stimulating that conversation is today our fundamental purpose at the Appalachian Trail Conservancy.

I believe the pages that follow—photographic documentation of the magic of the eastern mountains we all love—will persuade you that such a purpose is both noble and natural.

Ron J. Tipton
*Executive Director / Chief Executive Officer,*
*Appalachian Trail Conservancy*

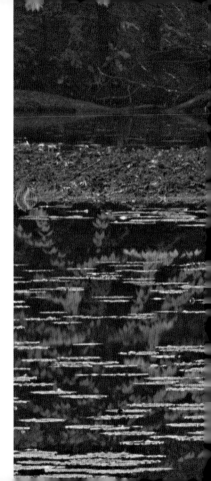

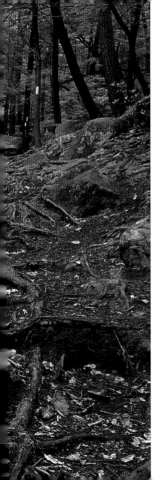

199

# L I S T   O F   P L A T E S

First published in the United States of America in 2017
by Rizzoli International Publications, Inc.
300 Park Avenue South
New York, NY 10010
www.rizzoliusa.com

Project Editor: Candice Fehrman
Book Design: Susi Oberhelman

 APPALACHIAN TRAIL
C O N S E R V A N C Y®

Appalachian Trail Conservancy
P.O. Box 807
Harpers Ferry, WV 25425

2017  2018  2019  2020 / 10  9  8  7  6  5  4  3  2  1

Printed in China

ISBN-13: 978-0-8478-5917-7

Library of Congress Catalog Control Number: 2016952484